Channeled Messages From Source

Daily Inspiration, Guidance, and Truth

By
Carrie Cardozo

Copyright © 2023 Carrie Cardozo

ISBN 13:

All Rights Reserved.

No part of this book may be reproduced in any form or by any electronic means including information storage and retrieval systems without written permission from the author except for the use of brief quotations in a book review.

To Maddie, Noah, and Bell,

You guys are my world! Thank you for navigating this crazy journey we call life with me!

I love you!

About These Messages

These messages can be read any way you choose. Looking for direction, ask your question with the book closed and open to the page.

Allow your day to begin or end with these daily messages from Source.

It's time to open, expand, and step into what you're meant to do with this life.

The path is yours, it's up to you to make of it what you desire.

Feel Inspired, Snap a photo, share it on your socials and tag me

It's time to move through the fear and step into your power.

The life you desire is on the otherwise of the pain you are causing yourself.

Step into the fear, release the pain and allow yourself to receive.

Relax into the moment.

Sit in the silence.

Feel the peace within.

Life is lived moment to moment but often one tries to plan, see and act in the past or future.

When you stop, bring your attention to now, one is able to be fully present.

That allows for true connection and harmony.

Walk with faith.

For when one walks with fear, struggle, and doubt are allowed into reality.

When struggle and doubt enter, the path one walks brings one farther from truth.

The power lies within you.

Your potential is determined by the level you hold that power.

Today, show yourself just how much potential you have!!

Let go of your old way of thinking.

Stop trying to fix the situation.

Surrender to the here and now.

The path before you is clear.

Your job is to take one step after another and trust the journey, not try to change it.

For you can't see the blessings that are coming.

Clear the mind.

Let the heart lead the way.

What is before you may feel big and overwhelming but that's just because you're seeing it through the eyes of the past.

Close your eyes and see it through your heart. Feel your way forward.

Walk with confidence.

Walk with trust.

Prepare for all the amazing things ready to show up in your life.

For this life is yours to create.

This life is simply waiting for you to catch up.

What will you create?

Trust is a state of being you can get to, but first, it must be practiced.

Practiced in the fear.

Practiced when you can't see the way.

Practiced even when it seems impossible.

Practiced most when there is no other option.

To get to the state of trust, one must let go of the human desire to control and lean into the soul's knowing and Universal guidance.

How can you practice trust?

You can do anything you desire in life, you simply must believe it.

You can have anything you choose in life, you simply must trust it.

This life is here for you to dream, align, and create but you often place limitations on yourself for lack of knowing.

This is not the Universe doing, this is your own creation. Where are you limiting yourself in life?

Open your eyes.

See the world clearly.

Don't let judgments and fears taint the beauty that exists around you.

The world is full of opportunities and choices. Your job is to explore them all.

Through these experiences, you're able to remember who you really are.

Relax into the moment.

Trust the process.

Let joy vibration run through your entire body.

Feel your soul emanating up and guiding you with its soft and gentle way.

For your journey is about to open to new possibilities.

Acceptance is not about giving up on one's dreams for what is present now.

Acceptance says you're not going to deny your circumstances or fight them but rather allow them to be.

Once acceptance is achieved then your circumstances have the ability to change.

Today, accept where you are at.

Stop resisting.

Lean in and let it be what it is.

Then, ask the Universe to show you your next step, knowing you will have all you desire, but not needing to see proof right now.

This is a powerful time for change. Embrace it!

You can not have what you continue to resist.

Open your heart.

Give love in plenty.

Have compassion for what you don't understand.

Accept all that you can see.

Open to flow and allow in what the Universe asks you to receive.

When you do, it will change your life.

Once the momentum is created let it flow.

Don't hold back, don't force it. Simply allow.

Today is a great day to witness where the momentum that you have created is shifting things in your life.

Recognize these shifts and celebrate them.

Peace is a state that is achieved within.

Presence is the path to achieve it.

You often spend much of your time focusing on the past or the future which creates anxiety and fear. Keeping you disconnected from the moment.

Today, focus on the present moment and allow the feelings of peace to fill your body and soul.

Walk with peace knowing that everything is in perfect order. For when you believe it, you begin to allow the Universe to create it.

You can not change what you do not acknowledge.

You can not shift what you are unwilling to see.

When you open yourself up to truth, the real transformation is available.

But only when you decide you are ready.

One must center oneself within the confines of one's thoughts before they are able to break free.

Only then can one truly understand the purpose of those thoughts and the impact they have..

Stand in the space you've created.

Breathe in the moment of now.

Rejoice in all that you are.

Trust in the next steps you are taking.

You are guided and supported in all ways.

Let the fear wash away as you look at all the possibilities.

Your doubts are not serving you.

This life is made up of all the things you tell yourself.

Today, let there be a new dialogue. Let there be a new wave of hope and excitement. Let there be a new energy around what's to come!

Walk with trust.

There is a light within that can not go out.

It might be dimmed.

It might be overpowered by shadows.

But it will never go out.

Walk with trust and that light will continue to shine brighter.

Go inward.

Sit in your energy.

Listen to your thoughts.

Feel into your heart space.

Hold space for yourself to be present.

Take a moment to honor what you need.

Release judgment and just allow.

Today marks another significant change if you give yourself the space to allow it.

Right now the times of change are upon us.

Things are shifting.

Space is opening up.

Your past is falling away.

The future is revealing itself.

Make space for new things in your life.

Let the energy flow in!

Let the energy of today open your eyes to all you can see and witness.

Allow today to create a shift that transforms who you are and how you show up in life.

Embrace the changes that follow as the Universe has a much bigger plan than even you could imagine.

It's a powerful time we are in. Stop trying to change the energy. Allow it to change you!

Fear not for what you don't understand.

Your guidance brings you to where you need to be and your truth takes you through it.

The only fear that truly exists is your lack of trust in yourself. For you are the only one who matters.

Today, stand in your own beliefs and your own truth and let your trust show you the way.

To hold trust is to be brave.

To accept help is to be strong.

To follow your truth is to be unshakable.

Let go of all that's holding you back and you will see your entire world change.

Today, let your fears show you the way forward.

Flow with the energy.

Move with your intuition.

Today is a day to allow yourself to be guided and to not force.

Often the energy can feel uncomfortable. This is not to be avoided. This is to be honored and used for awareness and change. Let today help to facilitate a deeper change.

Sit in peace.

Tap deep within and listen to that inner voice.

Feel that inner pull.

Allow all that is within to flow to the surface.

Open up your communication channels with yourself and dive deep into your truth.

Reflection is key.

Love is the most powerful energy on Earth.

It has the ability to heal, transform, and shift lives.

It's the one energy you are connected back to yet you often don't use it.

Today, tap into love.

Let it expand your heart.

Let it open you up to a deeper connection to truth.

Allow love to remind you of your purpose on Earth and just how powerful you are.

For love is all there is.

There is much to learn about yourself.

There is much to explore.

So often we become what others desire us to be and forget all about who we already are.

Today lean into who you desire to be and let go of all that others are projecting onto you.

It serves no one.

It's not about the progress you make. It's about the way you feel in each moment.

It's not about the end goal. It's about each individual step in your journey.

Stop trying to get to a certain place. Instead, bask in where you are right at this moment.

Don't compare.

Don't judge.

Simply rejoice every single day.

Don't take the things you've learned for granted.

Don't see the things you've done as small.

Each and every moment of your life has contributed to this very second right here.

This very second right here is all that matters. For it's in this moment that you are being your true self.

Be her.

See her.

Love her.

Experience all of her.

Allow her to show you all the beauty of her.

Center yourself in gratitude.

Witness how beautiful life is.

Then, share it with others.

The most powerful thing about life is whatever you focus on expands. As you navigate through your day don't forget this. Use this power to create a ripple effect of all that you love.

Relax

Breath

Surrender

All is being taken care of and there is nothing to fear.

There are many shifts unfolding right now and you have an opportunity for change.

As you move through the next couple of days, be very intentional in your actions and choices. Always move with alignment and ease.

That will show you which way to go.

When you become the focus of your life, all that surrounds you shifts to prioritize all that is needed and desired.

Prioritize yourself.

Become the center of your life.

Let the world revolve around you and you'll soon see everything lining up to respond to you. Then your life will completely change.

The path before you is open.

Take one step forward.

Lean into what comes and get ready for more.

Things are about to start shifting.

Stop using your fears and resistance as reasons not to move forward.

Stop using your struggles as examples why life isn't working out.

It's all in your hands.

It's how you navigate through what comes up that determines your success.

You can not have what you do not feel worthy of receiving.

Change that.

Whatever it is you desire will become yours when you know your value around it and believe you will have it.

You must believe.

Are you aware of the power you have in life?

Are you aware of all that is influenced by your thoughts, words, actions, and energy?

Today, witness the way the Universe responds to you, how life responds to you.

It truly is a beautiful thing.

You can have anything your soul desires.

You can have anything your human requires.

You can have everything you need.

But you must believe.

You can not achieve what you don't believe is possible.

Do you believe?

Open your heart and receive all the love that's being blessed upon you!

Open your heart and allow the world to show you all the good in it.

Open your heart and let those around you feel your love.

It's safe to open your heart!

Surrender to the moment.

Let your worries wash away.

Everything you've ever needed has been supplied to you as will this.

Let your heart open to receive and carry you forward into the greatest moments of your life.

All is as it should be.

Do you believe??

Before you take action, lean into your trust.

Before you stress, lean into your knowing.

Before you jump to fear, lean into your heart.

You always have all the answers inside of you. Are you listening?

When one opens up to great possibilities, great possibilities open up to you.

Arise and move forward in the vastness of all that awaits you. Let go of your fears. Accept the truth that you can have all that you dream of. For only then will it truly be possible.

It's waiting for you. Are you ready?

One can not enjoy the fruits of their labor till one steps up and takes responsibility.

Claim what you have power over and dive in to create it.

Open your heart to possibilities as there is so much to experience.

Yet you hold yourself back out of fear.

You restrict yourself out of doubt.

The universe is responding to you.

How will you show up today?

Laugh

Play

Tap into pure joy.

This shift in your vibration will enhance your mood, open your heart to receive, and magnetically attract things to you.

Let's shift the energy today.

The energy of the day is patience and trust.

There is much you are waiting on and even more you are wanting to do.

Today, lean into patience.

It's all unfolding in perfect timing.

Today, lean into acceptance.

Things are how they are for a reason.

Today, lean into trust.

There is something greater unfolding here and you will be given the way.

You are supported and being led. Do you believe?

What are you calling in and how can you practice trust?

Expand your belief.

Move beyond what you think is possible into the unimaginable.

Stretch yourself into the uncomfortable.

Allow the universe to show you what awaits.

Once you see the power you hold inside, you'll never underestimate what you have the ability to achieve.

Your soul came here to experience a life that allowed it to learn more about itself, to see what it was capable of, and to better express its truth.

That's not achieved by playing small or resisting expansion.

The more you tap into your power the deeper connection you have to your soul and the more fulfilling this life becomes.

Stop resisting what is being shown to you.

The uncomfortable is where the true alignment with your soul begins and the fullness of your power is explored!

Wait.

Be present.

The world is conspiring for you.

The Universe is expanding with you.

Everything's coming together in the most beautiful unfolding to support you.

Are you ready?

Stop

Close your eyes.

Take a deep breath.

Feel your heart beating.

Feel your body relax.

Allow your vibration to rise.

Feel the power of Source inside you.

Now make your move.

The expansions are upon us and there is so much magic in the air!

The clarity is being fed to you through your consciousness.

The power surrounds you through your connection.

The Universe bestows upon you all that you are capable of.

The path is being shown.

You have so much available to you, will you step in?

A fresh start is coming.

But first, you must release the baggage.

Cleanse the mind.

Clear the heart.

Connect to the soul.

Tap into the beauty that you hold and let it shine.

It's time to let go of the regret and the doubt.

Your job is not to hold onto the past. It's to honor and learn from it, as you lovingly let it go.

Only then can you change your future by shifting your focus and energy on who you desire to be, instead of who you were.

Close your eyes.

Breathe deep into your heart.

Open up your heart to love.

Allow all the past pain to flow through you and out.

Breathe deep into your heart for one last cleansing breath.

Open your eyes to the new possibilities of you and your life.

Sway with the breeze and let the sun hit your face.

The radiance of your being is desiring connection and activation from the earth.

We are moving into new times of self-expression and trust.

Connect with heart.

Connect with Earth.

Connect with all the power supporting your expression.

Then let the energy fill you.

Get used to feeling aligned.

Get used to feeling complete.

There is a bigger calling whispering in your ear.

Are you listening?

There is a loving voice guiding you forward.

Will you hear?

All that you came here to do is coming into your awareness right now.

Tune in to listen.

Tune in to hear.

Tune in and allow the flow to open you to greater possibilities.

There is so much to come.

The time has come to celebrate you!

To get honest with your achievements and to recognize where you are already living your dreams.

We can get lost in a narrow focus.

Today, I invite you to see your life from that Birds Eye view.

Look at all you've done.

Look at all you've created.

Look at all you've learned.

And celebrate YOU!

You can be the most powerful version of yourself at any moment.

Just choose it.

You can have everything you desire.

Just choose it.

You can make the grandest of changes in your life.

Just choose it.

Wherever you are at.

Whatever you have.

Whoever you are.

You are choosing it.

Today we make new choices.

What you are reaching for is achievable, but not until you truly believe.

Who you desire to be is attainable, but not until you let go of who you are now.

Things don't just happen to you. You must be the one to make them happen.

Today, what are you committing to showing up and creating?

You can't have what you're not willing to start.

You can't end what you aren't willing to let go of.

Oftentimes the only thing holding you back is YOU!

It's scary to let go when you aren't certain of what's to come, but you must be willing to lose what you have, to attain what it is you desire!

Where are YOU keeping yourself back?

The magic is in the flow.

We often push and force ourselves to make things happen and to achieve what we desire.

But the pure magic that truly creates is in the flow.

Connect to your heart.

Relax into your body.

Ground your energy.

Breathe deep into your sacral.

Activate that magic and flow. And watch all that you create!

You've come here to do something truly amazing.

To share

To be

To have

To love

It's time to step into all of it.

It's time to open your heart to all that you can be.

It's time to let the world see you.

It's time to no longer hide.

Today I ask you to be seen. To truly let others share in all that you are and all that you have the ability to be.

Light the world up with your truth and let your heart be revealed.

The world needs you!

Expansion is upon us and change is inevitable.

The heart is opening to new discoveries about oneself.

The soul is rising to partake in life even more powerfully.

The voice is strengthening to share one's message.

Your time is now.

You are needed.

You are important.

Will you step in?

The wait is over. Things are shifting.

What you thought would never happen is now happening.

What you thought was once impossible is now possible.

What you felt was only for others is now becoming yours.

But you must be strong.

You must work through the resistance.

You must navigate through any pain.

You must open your heart to believe in your truth.

You must be willing to step fully in and do the work.

What is coming is big.

What you've asked for is here.

Are you prepared?

The act of patience in one's life can transform reality.

Instead of counting the time that passes, one sinks into the energy of the moment.

Living life to the fullest.

Trusting that what is desired will come when it's meant to.

Today, tap into the energy of patience and trust and let go of marking time.

Dare to dream big and believe you can have it all.

What awaits you is higher than you think and more expansive than you can imagine.

Will you let yourself experience it all?

One small step each day brings you closer and closer to where you desire to be.

But you're not trusting that.

You desire big steps.

You desire massive movement daily or you don't believe it's happening.

The more you allow and flow, the stronger you become rooted in your feminine. The more you transform into your essence, the more pure alignment you receive and activate.

It's all coming together.

Everything you've asked for is coming in its own way.

Trust

Flow

Align

Allow

The perfect place for you is right here, exactly where you are right now.

We often try to resist what we are going through.

But you're here for a reason.

There is something you must experience.

Stop trying to fight it.

Surrender

Accept

Understand

Then shift.

It's working.

It's all working out.

It's all working out better than you could even imagine.

But are you holding the energy of it or are you doubting?

Are you certain of what's coming or are you doubting?

You decide your future.

Today is the day to start acting like it.

There is much you need to learn about the power you have in your life.

Every place you feel weak, insignificant like you have no control or have been forgotten... is where you can expand your understanding of your own power.

You are never out of power and there is nothing out of your control.

How you use it matters.

Remember that.

Fill your heart with love today.

For the people you care about.

For the things that you have.

For the life that you live.

Fill your heart with love today.

For the work that you've done.

For the things you have built.

For how far you have come.

Fill your heart with love today.

For the amazing person you are.

For having the heart to be true!!!

We are filling our hearts for you!

Step away from the pain and the hurt and the repeating patterns of disappointment.

Step away from feeling like you're not enough.

Step away from constantly questioning your worth and your readiness.

Step away from the fealing of failure.

None of those things are real.

Those things are perspectives from your mind. Beliefs from your past.

Tap into your heart.

Tap into your depth.

Breathe in your essence.

Activate your power.

See what's possible.

Believe in you.

Today is a day to activate a drive to achieve.

There is so much hidden wisdom held within you.

Quiet the mind.

Tune in.

Open the heart.

Ask to see.

Every answer you've ever needed is already inside.

Are you listening?

Want to see your truth?

Open your eyes. It's all around you.

It's in the people in your life.

It's in the words you hear as well as speak.

It's in the way your life flows.

It's in the money that you have (or don't).

It's the situations that show up.

It's in the way your day unfolds.

The Universe is always showing you your alignment and truth.

You're just not open to seeing or accepting it.

Only once you do, can you change it.

Be Still

Breathe

Wait

Observe

Nothing is accomplished through force that wasn't already intended through alignment.

Your struggle is created within.

Your resistance is a fear you hold.

Be Still

Breathe

Wait

Observe

Stop taking actions from fear and let your soul show you the way.

There is nothing you can't overcome.

Your mere desire to overcome something shows you are capable of doing so.

When there is chaos in your life, find the silence.

Don't fight.

Don't try to figure it out.

Don't push against it.

Lean into what's going on and find the silence.

For in the silence is the strength and the path through it.

Surrender....

Into the moment.

Into the emotions.

Into the thoughts.

There is much to observe about your life right now.

There is much to experience.

Don't let your emotions, your fears or your expectations remove or keep you from the importance of what you're going through.

Surrender and allow the Universe to show you all you need to know.

You are enough

You are more than enough.

You are all you'll ever need to be.

Already inside, you are that person.

Your job is to release what others have told you about yourself or made you feel.

Then remember who you are.

The importance of connection lies in the trust you build with yourself.

Any struggle

Any pain

Any fear

Any confusion

Can not withstand the trust held within.

Today focus on your inner connection and build your inner truth.

Watch it change your life.

The truth you are holding will shift the course of life as you know it.

But you're afraid to look within.

You're waiting for something big and grand.

But you'll never find it that way.

The truth you're holding is all you'll need. The grandness comes from acknowledging, accepting and sharing what lies within.

The totality of it is created in the sharing and unfolding of it into existence. Not while it's still held within.

Share your truth and let it fill the world with its fullness.

The world is waiting.

Expect Miracles

Expect the Best

Expect that everything you've ever wanted is on its way to you now.

There is nothing aligned for your soul that you can not have.

But your job is to believe it's coming.

Do you?

Peace in your heart.

Smile on your face.

Light in your eyes.

You attract everything you desire in life.

Start now!

Sink into the energy of truth.

Bathe in the energy of peace.

All around you, there are opportunities to see just how loved and cared for you are.

The world doesn't have to be a hard place.

You don't have to be scared.

Feel the energy you desire and allow it to emanate throughout your body.

You are loved.

You are supported.

Pause

Breath

What's being shown to you right now is all the expansion available to you!

What you're navigating through is all the potential that you have the ability to create with.

Pause

Breath

When you feel it in your heart, step in.

You light up this world.

Your energy is brilliant.

Your spirit is beautiful.

Your human is unique.

There is a very specific reason you are here.

To shine your light.

To share your love.

To offer your beauty.

Never forget it.

you've come here to experience the most magical life you could.

Are you doing that?

Your soul chose this life, this time, this way.

Lean into the experience.

Decide what you will place your focus on.

Live every single day with purpose.

This is your life.

Scarcity is a mindset.

But it is also an emotion.

It's a feeling that lies deep within your body. And that feeling is preventing abundance.

Tap into those emotions to help you understand why they are there.

Feel them and let them release.

Then open yourself up to appreciating.

That appreciation feeling allows you to activate your ability to receive.

It's time for you to open to receive.

You've come here to experience the most magical life you can.

Are you doing that?

Your soul chose this life, this time, this way.

Lean into the experience.

Decide what you will place your focus on.

Live every single day with purpose.

This is your life.

Clarity comes when you

let down your walls, stop making excuses, and allow yourself to see the truth.

Expansion comes when you

implement and step into what's been shown.

Are you willing to expand?

You can not rush what you desire by begging, pleading, and getting frustrated.

You don't manifest by desiring more.

To call in what you're waiting for, align with it, know that it's going to happen, believe that it's already here.

Then patiently wait in trust.

Mark this day down as the day things change.

You are opening up to much more in your life.

More connection.

More allowing.

More trusting.

Mark this day down as the day you believe in yourself.

You are no longer doubting, questioning, or judging.

More loving.

More choosing.

More believing.

This day gets to be the day YOU make a change and decide that you deserve MORE and you are going to show up for YOU!

I am ready for more!

The sun shines brightly to remind you of your brilliance.

The stars stand powerfully to remind you to lead.

The moon casts its glow to guide you in your darkness.

All around you, the world is reminding you of your power, of your purpose, and of just how supported you are.

Which aspect, the sun, the stars, or the moon do you most resonate with and which is it time you remind yourself of?

You tend to count the days as you wait for time to pass and for the things that you desire to come into your life.

Today I invite you to stop counting.

Lean DEEP into the moment.

Recognize all that each second offers you.

Everything that you have the ability to enjoy in every single moment.

It's often easy to see the importance of a moment of time or a single passing instance when looking back and reflecting.

Today, start seeing the importance BEFORE the time goes by.

The passage of time means nothing.

It doesn't mean you'll grow.

It doesn't mean things will change.

It doesn't mean you'll get what you desire.

It's simply a marker of space.

YOU are the one to make that time mean something.

Your thoughts create an idea, your actions create a change and your acknowledgment of the growth creates momentum for more.

You're being asked to step into the most powerful time in your life, but you must step in.

Nothing else is going to create it for you.

Not time.

Not another person.

Not even fate.

Right now it's all in your hands.

What will you do?

Your passion is your compass.

Your desires are your fuel.

Your purpose here is to show up and be the most authentic version of yourself.

When you're vibrating at the highest frequency and attracting the greatest manifestations your life comes into perfect alignment and your soul is fulfilled.

The world around you is applauding your glory. Are you seeing it?

There are things every day showing you just how amazing and magical you are. But oftentimes you can get caught up in worrying you're not enough, or questioning yourself.

Today, just for one day, pretend that you're amazing. That there is no one else like you. That everything you do is perfect. That it's all working out for you. That the world is supporting your every decision. That everything is showing up to help you succeed.

Because it's all true anyway.

So go be amazing today.

♥

Reflection into your beliefs and values can bring insight into the direction you're heading.

Feeling into your emotions can tell you why.

Everything you need to shift in life is healed inside of you.

Today let it come into your awareness.

Shine your light.

Use your voice.

Open your heart.

Don't be afraid to let the whole world see all of who you are!

They deserve it!!

Share something about yourself today!!

Willing yourself to success will not work.

Open your heart.

Dig into the pain and the resistance.

Understand what you are protecting.

And surrender into it.

Feel it and accept it.

Then be brave enough to let it go.

What is being asked of you is an opportunity for a deeper connection to self and to spirit.

Your soul yearns for expression. To be able to speak, to share, to flow through life in its own magic and glory.

Let it be free.

Give it permission to fly!

Contemplation can get you stuck in the mind, thus allowing fear or doubt to overtake you.

Release the need to figure things out and tap into your inner knowing,

Your intuition is always on.

It guides you in the moment. It leads you where you need to be.

Today, let go of the NEED to figure it out and let your inner knowing show you the way.

Walk with trust.

Surrender into the moment.

Let the fear leave your body.

Relax back into FLOW.

Today marks a moment in time when you are no longer questioning.

The moment you are no longer resisting.

The moment when you are no longer controlling.

Today you are moving in trust and knowing that your footsteps are leading the way.

Where once you were small, you now are big.

Where once you were afraid, you are now trusting.

Where once you were limiting, you are now expanding.

Your soul chose this journey because of all that it was going to experience and grow. Stop restricting the growth. Lean into the moments, even the uncomfortable ones, and allow your soul to be in all the glory that life is offering it.

When you release the resistance you allow the soul to flow!

What once seemed overwhelming is now the reality of what you are living.

The growth that you are able to achieve in life can feel impossible when looking forward.

When looking back you see how you were able to do it and the effect it has on your life.

Today, take a moment to look back.

Notice what once was just a thought or a desire is now part of your norm.

CELEBRATE all that you have accomplished and let the energy of that celebration build your trust and fuel your movement forward.

The soul knows.

The energy has the map.

The spirit is the force to follow.

While the human is what causes the disruption in the journey.

Where are you letting your human lead and ignoring the soul, the energy, and the spirit?

Walk with trust.

Lean into your faith.

All that appears before you is meant for you in this moment now.

What comes your way is meant to help you.

Try not to resist.

Try not to push it away.

Embrace this time in your journey.

Trust and you shall know.

Believe and you shall see.

Waiting to be shown to tap into a greater level of faith is what keeps the non-believers from activating higher levels of consciousness.

Your inner truth is what leads you in this life.

Nothing more is needed.

One can not enter into trust when one is still focused on the past.

Clear what is holding you back and allow all that your soul knows to guide you on your journey today.

There is a light that shines all around you.

It guides you and allows others to find you!

Can you see it?

This light comes from within. But every time you are in fear or doubt, you turn the brightness down.

The more fear you hold the dimmer and dimmer it gets till no one can see it.

Today is about turning that light back up.

Tap into your heart, hold joy, give love, and receive blessings. This lets your light shine.

One can not force results.

Results come simply from pure alignment and the knowing when, where, and how to show up.

This knowing is held deep within.

Quiet the ego and the knowing will emerge to show you the way.

You're stepping into a new phase in life.

Doors are opening and your heart is guiding you to where it desires to be.

Open your heart.

Let go of fear and past pain.

Listen to what it's asking of you.

Lean into the JOY that is held within this experience and let yourself truly live!

Walk with grace as you enter into the new and the unknown.

Each and every step is validation for your life and your success. Don't let the small things hold you back.

There are great things awaiting you that only you can achieve.

Walk with grace as you travel this life knowing that each step is divinely guided.

You are here to do great things, it's time you let yourself provide them.

One must believe in oneself before others can believe in them too.

One must share what's in the heart before others can feel the love too.

Everything in life starts within. In order for anything to be truly built and sustained it must originate within you first, or the existence of it will waver.

Open your heart and let the joy flow in.

Stop thinking about the past.

Stop wishing it were here.

Forward is the direction you are heading and the view is astounding.

Let yourself LOVE life.

Let yourself lean into PURE Joy.

Give yourself permission to truly LIVE!

Life is not trying to hold you back or keep you down.

It's giving you an opportunity to step into fate.

But fate is big.

It's often expansive.

It asks for power and presence.

When you let go and let fate lead your life the things you've been struggling with resolve themselves,

But you have to be willing to let them go so they become what is necessary to align your life with a greater plan.

Let go and let fate lead.

You have all the power in this situation.

Every thought.

Every step.

Every action.

But are you using it?

Are you trusting?

You're praying that Source (God, Universe) comes in and fixes it for you.

But YOU have the power, the wisdom, and the will to shift all of it yourself.

Close your eyes and open your heart.

Feel it beating.

Understand what's blocking you.

Open up and allow that to leave.

Follow the knowing that lies beneath the fear.

It's all in your hands, but you must believe it!

Walk with me.

Feel my hand in yours.

Notice our steps aligning.

Hear our breaths syncing.

Trust that I'm with you through all of this.

Oftentimes it feels like you travel this life alone.

You don't.

I'm always with you.

(You know who this is from!)

The heart knows what the mind won't accept.

The mind fears what the heart desires.

The truth lies between the two.

Clear the fear.

Release the emotions.

Tap into the heart.

Open to all the truth.

You came here to stand out, to be different.

You came here to cause a shift.

You can't do that if you're hiding behind your fears and insecurities.

Say the words.

Share the post.

Speak up and voice your truth.

They are waiting.

As you step forward into the unknown I invite you to shift your focus.

The unknown isn't a space to be uncertain about what's unfolding in life.

The unknown is a void in which you get to decide who you are, how you show up, and what you create.

This unknown is a space for you to become, for you to intend, and for you to receive.

The unknown is for you to shift to known.

Awaken to the possibilities that your path holds.

Remove doubt, fear, and lack as you step into the unknown.

What comes before you is meant to expand you.

What feels like resistance is an indication of that expansion.

What appears in front of you is an opportunity for more.

Right now is a time for greatness. Don't let your human conditioning stop the momentum.

Embrace all of it.

What we can't see is often what we fear the most.

What we can't process is what we feel around it.

Today as the storm arises, feel into all that's coming up.

Sit with it.

Allow all that needs to pass to do so.

It won't last forever.

The emotions you are feeling are bringing you full circle.

This discomfort you're facing is here for the clearing.

What's being activated is a new way of being.

It's all working together.

What once was, isn't serving.

But what's coming in isn't here yet.

Sit in the unknown and let the discomfort show you what to release.

This is a space for growth.

Not a space to fear.

Throughout life, there are choices we have to make.

Big choices often come with deep work.

The process in which this work is done varies.

You can choose to stay in the resistance.

Or

You can walk with faith.

There are many things in life you can not explain.

They often don't need explanations.

Choose to trust and continue forward.

The things you struggle over often become the things that are least important along the way.

While oftentimes you feel like you have no control in a situation, you almost always do.

Before you came here you created a plan.

While here you choose your focus.

You make choices every day.

Although the world can feel out of control and scary, everything is actually very much in control.

Lean into your center and ground into your power.

It's all unfolding as it should.

One must be aware of the power one holds.

The strength in the soul is often undiscovered.

The connection with the self is often misunderstood.

Reconnecting with one's faith leads to a revitalization of the memory one holds of past, present, and future.

Release the unknown and remember the truth.

One must open one's heart to acceptance and allow the truth to flow.

Never hurting.

Never pain.

Just pure knowing.

But once that truth is released, resistance is often activated.

The human fears and resistance is created.

Once one realizes the human has NO control, the resistance can dissipate.

But you let the human lead. You allow it.

Decide there is no room for pain and allow only knowing to arise.

Knowing for oneself and only self.

Resist the need to heal all when one's only need is to fully heal oneself.

Then the true cause of the pain is gone.

This is a time of deep sorrow.

It doesn't have to be.

Tap into truth and activate a new level of awareness, then share that... Not the pain.

The breakdown in communication is a direct reflection of an inability to truly listen.

When you get out of your own energy and fears you can hear what others are experiencing.

When you can truly hear, you can see what is unfolding for yourself.

Remove this energy of being blind to life and no longer see through your filter.

Tap in and see through your heart.

What the world needs now is love.

What the world is asking for is compassion.

What the world is looking for is acceptance.

No more judgment.

No more criticism.

No more fear.

Open your hearts and let the world feel your truth, let the energy from your soul shift the vibrations around you.

We need more soul and less fear-based energy.

Be at peace.

Be content.

Flow

Nothing needs to be forced.

Everything is coming to you.

Tap into your heart and witness that power and the beauty you have within.

That power is what leads you to your next steps.

That power is what is needed.

Putting a label on money gives it a meaning.

Let it just be.

It's energy, nothing more.

Would it be wrong to desire an overload of love?

Would it be bad to ask for more and more peace?

Your connection and attachment to money is what's giving it a feeling of being wrong.

Not the money.

You're here to serve.

That doesn't mean for nothing.

Your service is what you share with others.

Your payment, as you call it, is the money you receive from it.

Today, let go of your resistance to money.

Today, decide it means nothing.

Today, recognize that nothing you desire is wrong.

It's all energy you are choosing to receive.

Receive it!

Walk with truth.

Let it open your heart.

Allow it to penetrate your soul.

For you came here to live and experience the truth that lies within.

You came here to be an expression of your truth in every aspect of your life.

When you allow your truth to lead, your life becomes perfectly aligned with the vibration of your soul.

The heart speaks when it opens.

The soft whispers move through your body and can be felt with every breath.

The voice of the heart is guiding you into the unknown. Yet the unknown becomes familiar when you stop questioning and doubting.

Let down your guard and let your heart lead you forward.

See what is beyond your reach and take it.

Often life is misunderstood. You think that what you can see, beyond what you have, is only available for a few.

It's not.

What you can see, the things your heart desires, are truly meant for you.

But you doubt it.

If you can see it, you can have it.

Today, start believing it.

Decide what it is that you see, that you have been feeling is out of your reach, and realize that you are moments away from having it too.

Walk with the truth that everything is exactly how it should be.

Move with the knowing that your intuition is leading you.

Expand with the understanding that you can have and be anything you desire.

This life was created for you to live the fullest expression of all that's possible for you.

It's time you start to do that!

The coming of age is upon us.

A time when big shifts and quick transformations happen.

A time when many more will rise.

Those who have the power may lose it if that power isn't pure.

Open your heart and let your power activate.

Open your throat and let your truth be heard.

Expand your energy and let others feel your love.

Dive deep within and clear the fear.

A time has come when those who truly hold their power will rise and experience the world in an entirely different way.

Are you one of them?

When you walk with trust in life, new experiences arrive.

When you walk in truth, your world reorganizes to support you.

When you walk in power, your world becomes your own.

Trust, truth, and power are the energies one must hold to transform life.

Spirit speaks to you in every moment.

Through the whisper in the trees.

Through the beating of your heart.

Through the animals that cross your path.

Are you listening?

So often you wait for a dramatic download or a sudden event to tune into what's being asked.

Every day there is guidance.

Every moment there is connection.

The more you recognize it, the more you'll see it.

The more you see it, the more supported you are.

Do not doubt your support for it's all around you. Your ability to hear and acknowledge it will shift the level at which you accept it.

Once you're tapped into your true self, everything changes.

You have the ability to access new levels of being.

You understand things clearly.

Life shifts immediately.

Today your soul is speaking to you and opening up glimpses into that energy of your true self.

Your job is to feel it and hold it.

True connection comes from a feeling and a knowing.

True connection comes from an internal shift into awareness and consciousness.

Get out of your head and into your true awareness of self.

Then let that inner feeling secure your knowing and connection.

There is a calmness deep within you, whispering encouragement and guidance.

There is wisdom bubbling up locked inside your energy.

Open to what's within and allow your soul to lead you.

Today is about trust, connection, and self.

What once was, no longer has to be.

You hold the power to step into a new truth, to activate a new vibration, and to live a new level of being at any moment.

Let that moment be now.

Let go of old beliefs and clear the low vibrational energy as you let your soul lead the way.

The greatness you hold is locked just behind your beliefs.

Let go of what you should do and step excitedly into what you know is possible.

It's all your choice.

Lean in.

Expand your capacity to trust.

Withstand the need to shrink back or hide.

Acknowledge the fact that you're ready to play big.

The Universe is reorganizing things to make this the most powerful month yet.

But, you must listen…

to the inner pull.

to the heart.

to all your power.

Do not play small.

Do not let fear direct you.

It's time to go all in.

Are you ready?

The desire for more is normal.

Expansion and growth are a necessity in life.

The NEED for more is not.

Expand from a place of wholeness and that expansion, in all areas, will flow naturally.

There is nothing you lack, but there are many things you can gain.

You become the most beautiful version of who you are by accepting all of you.

There are many things that will be revealed to you as you walk with trust.

But these revelations are meant to show you the beauty that you hold within and what's stopping you from embracing them.

Trust.

Let this move you deep within.

Then embrace all of it and let others see it as well.

There is a turning point you are coming upon. Don't let your fear hold you back.

Jump in and let your soul guide you as you move.

Let your fear show you what to step into and never look back.

There is always a way to witness everything you are experiencing in life from two perspectives.

One that judges finds fault, and sees the limitations of it all. Causing one to coil back, become stuck, and regress.

Or... the one where you see how it's serving, what shifts it's creating, and how expansive it can be.

It's seeing it through the eyes of truth instead of a filter of fear and lack.

Today, you get to decide to see life through a new lens.

The old lens is broken.

Now only the clear lens will lead you forward.

Shift your perspective and see how life opens up for you.

The grace in which you move through life offers the world a glimpse into who you are and what you stand for.

The power you hold while offering that grace lets the world know what you are capable of.

Hold them both!

I invite you to stand in your truth, remember who you are, and let all of the world see your power.

You didn't come here to experience life like anyone else, so stop comparing your journey to theirs.

You have to release the belief that one ideology is fitting and true for all.

Each of you has your own experience, your own expansion, and your own truth to follow. Let that be done.

One can not advance in life through another's beliefs.

The path before you is created in your truth. The road you walk will determine your outcome.

Choose the one that brings you the most inner fulfillment in life and you'll never be in the wrong place.

Your experience is designed to achieve exactly what your soul brought you here to have.

Let it be true to you.

Awaken the soul to the pure essence that exists within and allow the world to see you.

The shifts, the upleveling, and the abundance are pure fire.

There is more to all of this than you realize.

More soul.

More power.

More responsibility.

The actions you take in life are just a part of the great unfolding.

The energetics, the truth, the trust in what's before you, hold much more frequency than any action you can be taking.

As you lean into new territories it's important your energetic vibration is a match for what is unfolding.

Your frequency delivers a message to the universe. Then your actions become the vessel in which your request is delivered.

Stop worrying about how much you're doing and start tapping into the frequency to hold.

Once you are a perfect match, the actions will be shown to you.

You came forth into this life to experience the most profound transformation.

To be the greatest expression of your gifts and abilities.

Yet, you question and doubt.

You wonder if you are good enough. If you can really have it all. Be who you desire.

Your job is not to ponder the relevance of your life. To question if you are enough. To compare yourself to others.

And you most definitely did not come forth to duplicate what's already been done.

Your life was chosen to live uniquely through your own vibrational expression as you live, tapped into your highest frequency.

Go be that amazing spirit.

The path to expansion is created with opportunities.

You can embark on each one or you can pass them right by.

The choice is up to you.

Each opportunity you partake in brings new levels of self-awareness and a shift in the path, causing that path to hold more and more opportunities, each one expanding you at a faster rate.

Each one you pass by creates another opportunity of a similar vibration to be enjoyed.

You can continue to create similar opportunities as long as you keep walking.

Or, you can continue to build your self-awareness and growth through rapid expansion with every opportunity you engage in.

That choice is yours.

The guidance you need lies just beyond your ability to set aside your fears, to get out of your logic, and to trust in yourself.

So often you search outside for answers for your truth.

All the while holding everything you need deep inside.

Today clear your channels and follow what your inner knowing is telling you!

Surrender into the potency and witness the discord.

Your body is simply fighting the expansion it knows it's time to make.

Relax into the moment and trust that the stretching is creating a ripple effect for years to come.

Feel

Let Go

Let the energy guide you forward.

Walk with certainty that everything is working out.

Walk with confidence that you are being guided every single step of the way.

Walk with the knowing that what you desire is coming to you.

For everything you think is becoming your truth and your truth becomes your reality.

Stop looking for permission.

Stop waiting for confirmation.

This life you are living is meant to be lived on your terms.

Show up and live it in the most extraordinary way and watch how things shift.

The wills of your soul are being felt.

You are being moved to feel, to love, to express, and to desire.

This activation that is happening is lifting you up and aligning you deeper with your truth and with all that is within.

Let the emotions be felt.

Let the voice be heard.

Let the desires be met.

For your soul is leading you to the perfection your human came here to achieve!

And it's beautiful.

The world is abound with opportunities for your wisdom to be shared.

The world is engrossed in all that you have to offer.

Step forward and share.

Let the world see your light.

Let the world hear your voice.

Show the world exactly who you are.

It's waiting.

The confidence you have in yourself and the connection are directly related.

The more connected you feel the more confident you become.

The ties that bind you in this life are directly related to the disconnection you feel.

Pause

Breath

Relax into your body.

The deeper you connect. The deeper you feel. The deeper your trust in yourself becomes.

Your connection builds the platform you need for success.

You are on the presuppose of something truly amazing.

Can you feel it?

Everything before you is available to you.

Anything you choose is able to be created.

You are at a time in life when all the power is available to you. It lies in your hands.

The future that you desire has the ability to be shifted into the exact circumstances that you need to create everything.

But you have to be willing to do it.

You have to be able to hold all of it.

Reality and availability are shifting and being given back to the holder. With this power, life becomes exactly what you make it.

Tap into your power and decide how you will use it.

Desire to change lies deep within your heart.

Resistance to change lies deep within the subconscious.

Your ability to change relies on your connection to your heart, your commitment to accessing parts of your subconscious that are keeping you stuck, and your willingness to do the deep work.

The power for great transformation lies inside of you!

But only you can access it and only when you're tired of being stuck in the same place.

Softly

Slowly

You wake up to the power of you.

You come back to your inner truth.

You let go of others' expectations.

You trust in your own inner strength and beauty.

Softly

Slowly

You let yourself shine.

Softly

Slowly

About Carrie

Carrie is a Soul Prophet, a Master Psychic Healer, and a Psychic Activator.

She is a leader in the psychic world and known for her ability to activate everyone who comes to her with their UNIQUE SOUL-aligned gifts.

Carrie works with experts, authorities, and leaders in their field to teach them how to open, connect, and activate their gifts and understand how to use them with power, integrity, and accuracy in their business.

Her sessions are one of a kind and will leave you in a new vibration and stepping into your power.

If you're ready to open up your world to energy, hold your power, and access a new level of psychic abilities, Carrie is your psychic.

Find her @CarrieCardozo or www.CarrieCardozo.com

www.ingramcontent.com/pod-product-compliance
Lightning Source LLC
LaVergne TN
LVHW011913080426
835508LV00007BA/509